Rome Travel Guide:

The Ultimate Rome, Italy Tourist Trip Travel Guide

By

Angela Pierce

Table of Contents

Introduction 5

Part 1. Places to Visit in Rome 7

   1. Piazza Navona 7

   2. Parioli and Flaminio 10

   3. Tridente 12

   4. Colosseum and Capitoline Hill 14

   5. Ghetto 16

   6. The Vatican and Prati 18

   7. Aventino 20

   8. Trastevere 22

   9. Gianicolo and Monteverde 23

   10. EUR 25

   11. Via Vittorio Veneto 27

   12. Ostiense and San Paolo 28

   13. Pigneto and San Lorenzo 30

   14. Monti and Esquilino 31

   15. Salario and Trieste 33

   16. San Giovanni 35

   17. Ostia 37

Part 2. Night Life in Rome 39

Conclusion 40

Thank You Page 41

Rome Travel Guide: The Ultimate Rome, Italy Tourist Trip Travel Guide

By Angela Pierce

© Copyright 2015 Angela Pierce

Reproduction or translation of any part of this work beyond that permitted by section 107 or 108 of the 1976 United States Copyright Act without permission of the copyright owner is unlawful. Requests for permission or further information should be addressed to the author.

This publication is designed to provide accurate and authoritative information in regard to the subject matter covered. This work is sold with the understanding that the publisher is not engaged in rendering legal, accounting, or other professional services. If legal advice or other expert assistance is required, the services of a competent professional person should be sought.

First Published, 2015

Printed in the United States of America

Introduction

Rome may not be built in a day, however one can unquestionably fall in love with the beauty of the city in a single day. The magnificence, glory, history, architecture will make the beholder travel through time and live in the era of greatness. The echoes of Roman Empire can still be heard in the city premises; the clash of swords, arguments of senators, battle cries, political barges, artistic pleasures, philosophic tendencies, strife for inventions, etc. makes Rome the microcosmic predecessor of the modern world. Furthermore, the moment you enter the city, the aura around it will penetrate into the soul procreating extravagant benevolence. If you are planning to visit Rome then make sure to cover all the areas, without missing any part of its history. The following information gives essence of Rome with region wise categorization so that visitors cannot miss a thing.

The climate of Rome

Rome's climate is not as diverse as its history. A typical subtropical-Mediterranean climate is observed with not so warm summers. The conditions do not go to extremes enabling visitors from other countries to get acclimatized to the weather with quick succession.

Part 1. Places to Visit in Rome

If you are planning to visit Rome then make sure to cover all the areas, without missing any part of its history. The following information gives essence of Rome with region wise categorization so that visitors cannot miss a thing.

1. Piazza Navona

This region famous for its ancient competition arena over time changed into a piazza built on Stadium of Domitian. Navona resonates with art and architecture based on Baroque which was prevalent artistic style during the 16th century. Interestingly, the present structure also resembles that of open stadium with rectangular form and rounded corners. The place is made accessible exclusively through foot which shows the enthusiasm of the Historians and the Government to safeguard their history with minutest details. The standout for Piazza Navona is the existence of three exuberant fountains:

Fontana dei Quattro Fiumi famously known as Fountain of the Four Rivers is situated at the centre of the piazza with an Egyptian obelisk at the centre surrounded by river gods representing four rivers of four continents namely, Nile, Ganges, Rio de la Plata and Danube.

La Fontana del Moro, The Moor fountain is present at the southern end of piazza with beautiful architecture and patterns. A moor standing on a conch shell is shown having a fight with dolphin.

Fontana del Nettuno, The fountain of Neptune at the northern end depicts sea god Neptune and his allies battling with sea creatures, the centre of attraction being Neptune accompanied by horse.

Apart from the fountains, Navona is known for its Baroque styled **church of St. Agnes** with intense architectural details, frescoes, etc. It is opposite to the fountain of four rivers and can be easily identified because of its magnanimous nature. In addition, **Pantheon** with oculus beaming sun rays which illuminate the entire hall of gods is a major attraction in Navona district.

Restaurants & shopping: As piazza is world renowned tourist destination, there is no scarcity of restaurants and bars. The best shopping place in Navona is Via del Governo Vecchio where there are many cafes, restaurants, shopping destinations. Tourists need not move a muscle as everything is available at close and visible distances. La Boticella, Ristorante Panzirone, Seaside Roma, Bernini Ristorante, La Pace Del Palato, and many more restaurants provide evocative recipes which do not leave the heart even after exiting the city of Rome.

2. Parioli and Flaminio

These regions are known for the parks and the famous Villa Borghese gardens which is its focal point. In addition, there is a deviation from historical presence in these localities. Visitors with children find it most amusing to visit this area as children have freedom and multiple options to obtain entertainment starting from play areas (like Casino di Rafaello), puppet theatres and ending with the great Casa del Cinema.

Villa Borghese gardens occupy a total space of 148 acres. There are many villas like the grand Villa Borghese, Villa Giulia, Villa Medici, etc. The gallery of Borghese is established inside the Villa Borghese which contains a collection of sculptures and paintings. The Galleria Nazionale d'Arte Moderna is also located on the grounds of the gardens which contain paintings of 19th to 20th century Italian artists.

Ponte Milvio, "The Lovers' Bridge" is well known among young lovers. Furthermore, it is known for antique supplies available over 200 stands. Various antique pieces are available in this area and definitely arouse interest among collectors.

Auditorium Parco della Musica of Flaminio is a music complex visited by over one million spectators a year with three major concert halls. Sala Petrassi, Sala Sinopoli, Sala Santa Cecilia attract the hearts of music zealots across the world making visitors to rush to this complex.

Restaurants & shopping: The restaurants and shops around the two regions are relatively cheap when compared to Navona district as the locality is not completely commercial and the neighborhood is friendly.

3. Tridente

Tridente is complex of roads in the form of a trident which derived its name because of its three pronged roads through Via di Ripetta, Via del Babuino and Via del Corso.

Piazza de Spanga – The Spanish steps overflow with Romans and tourists alike and it contains a central piece of The Ugly Boat and Keats-Shelly Memorial House which contains details about 19th century literature giants.

Piazza del Popolo retains its original Roman fervor struggling through ages of change and modification. The famous twin churches Santa Maira di Montesanto, Santa Maria di Miracoli and the Flaminio obelisk are major tourist places for every Roman visitor.

The Trevi Fountain is a complex artistic wonder which occupies an entire side of Palazzo Poli which focuses on the theme of Neptune led by Tritons with seahorses.

The Quirinal Palace conducts musical concerts on New Year's day and is famous for change of guards on every

Sunday. The palace was held as residence for Popes and King of Italy. However, the residential allowance of the palace was sojourn due to lot of renovations by famous artists.

Restaurants & shopping: Tridente is well-known for its local styled restaurants and shopping malls who try to preserve and spread their traditions in the form of recipes and shopping accessories. Enoteca Regionale Palatium, Colline Emiliane, etc are famous restaurants in Tridente.

4. Colosseum and Capitoline Hill

Colosseum is an amphitheatre built at the centre of the city of Rome. Needless to say it is the most popular of the Roman monuments and most people around the world know about it to a certain extent. Annually millions of visitors come to watch this monument which justifies its construction and effort.

The Forums represent the ancient administrative and public centers of Rome. After demolition and calamities fewer forums are intact and show the splendor of ancient Roman Empire.

The Palatine is mythological birth place of Rome where Remus and Romulus were raised by a she-wolf. Today it is a famous open museum vibrating the annals of Roman civilization.

The Capitoline Museums are one of the oldest museums around the world with myriad of collections like art works, bronze statues, and archeological relics. The statue of Emperor Constantine is another attractive aspect of the museums. Furthermore, the museums are interconnected by the help of underground tunnels leading to the forums. In addition these museums offer a roof-top café namely Palazzo Caffarell's terrace which gives a fantastic view of the city.

Restaurants & shopping: Celio is a small neighborhood behind the coliseum where there are many shops and unrecognized restaurants famous for their local food. There are wide ranges of shops from shoe repair shops to book repair shops. Fascinatingly, most tourists are unaware of this place and spend extra money for nearby places.

5. Ghetto

Ghetto of Rome is built close to the river Tiber and was under constant attack as history suggests. However, there are many historical monuments built around the place for which tourists visit Rome.

Fountain of the tortoises is affiliated with Romantic story which predates to 16th century and was believed to be built overnight without assistance. The fountain depicts four young men assisting four tortoises present in each direction to climb the basin.

The Tiber Island also known as the stone ship is associated with healing properties and people believe that their ailments are resolved by visiting the island.

The ruins of Portico Octavia originally meant to abode deities Juno and Jupiter; later it was turned to market place, ceremonial grounds, etc. Today, it resembles varied customs followed during ages yet retaining its original status.

The theatre of Marcellus is a functional amphitheatre which resembles the coliseum but on observation the difference is noted. Artists from different music academies and cultural institutions perform in this historic theatre during summer.

The synagogue was meant to be visible from every part of the city during the time of its construction. However, it is now popular for being the largest synagogue in Europe.

Restaurants & shopping: La Taverna del Ghetto, Giggetto, Nonna Betta, Al pompiere are well known restaurants in the region of ghetto. Comparatively, the region is less known for its shopping complexes yet it offers few shopping zones spread around the region.

6. The Vatican and Prati

If you visit Rome and leave without entering the Vatican, then there is literally no use in travelling to Rome. The Holy state administered and ruled by Pope. It is an encapsulated state with population of 842. Nonetheless, visitors entering Vatican are huge and most of them strive to have their presence during the ceremonies given by the Pope himself on Sundaes and festive seasons.

Vatican gardens can be visited with certain restrictions and access is possible only through a touring group. The access is given for only two hours and the visitor is escorted out of the garden if the time limit exceeds. However, those two hours can make the visitor peaceful as the place is filled with benevolence and pleasing designs further enhance calmness of mind.

St. Peter's Basilica is a master work of architecture by Renaissance artists and sculptors. It also houses the famous sculpture of Pietà and other high end artworks which keep inspiring many onlookers and enthusiasts.

The Sistine Chapel is the abode of Pope inside the Vatican; it is also famous to contain painting "The Last

Judgment". Another interesting aspect is the ceiling of Sistine Chapel designed by one of the masters of Renaissance.

Vatican museums are distributed within the boundaries of the city with vast collection of history, art, architecture, literature, etc. It would take days to comprehensively attend each display item. However, these museums do not disappoint as the places themselves are full of dignified wisdom which gets further enhanced by addition of other details.

Restaurants & shopping: Prati is the shopping destination which is exquisitely maintained around the walls of the Vatican. The streets and places are kept so clean and in addition, they are safe because of their reachable distance to stern Vatican legislation. Prati offers food, shopping, etc for everyone's need and requirement.

7. Aventino

Aventino district offers more aesthetic pleasure rather than historic knowledge and contains famous gardens like the rose garden and the garden of oranges. Nonetheless, archeological enthusiasts find this place useful because of the presence of certain historical monuments.

The temple of Portunus is well maintained fortunate survivor of ancient Rome dedicated to the god Portunus. It was used as church during the middle ages. The site has restricted access and tourists are allowed during 1st and 3rd Sundays of every month guided by registered accompanist.

The baths of Caracalla are reminders of daily habits and physical maintenance of the ancient Romans. In addition, the public baths functioned like community centers where people used to have conversations making them closer to each other.

Mouth of truth displayed in the Basilica of Santa Maria is famous because of stories related to it. People believe that the Bocca della Verità bites anyone who speak lies while keeping their hand in its mouth.

Restaurants & shopping: Aventino is known for its hotels and restaurants because tourists flock this area during festive seasons. Pizzeria da Remo, Ristorante le Mani in Pasta, Sushisen, Spirito di Vino, Taverna dè Mercanti, etc are well known restaurants and taverns available for visitors in Aventino.

8. Trastevere

Trastevere is mostly known for its murals, piazzas and botanical garden, along with regular shopping options and highly crowded restaurants. The reason for this is; Trastevere is located at the heart of the city.

9. Gianicolo and Monteverde

Gianicolo is considered as one of the best romantic spots around the world. The major reason being, the region is built on a hill which rises high enabling to view majority of Rome. In contrast, Monteverde is full of villas which turn the mind into more aristocratic setting.

Villa Pamphili offers park of 9 kilometers perimeter which gives a bird's eye view of the surroundings. This park is Rome's biggest in terms of area. The park is famous for providing excellent terrace view of villa Algardi.

Temple of Bramante was built during the high Renaissance with cylindrical shell of 4 meters with outside colonnade with admirable dome. The structure of the dome went few renovations through ages for its suitable sustenance. However, this temple precisely depicts the greatness of Renaissance art and architecture.

The fountain of Acqua Paola otherwise known as Janiculum Fountain is a massive fountain resembling a Roman building. Dragons and eagles are found in most places referring to the Borghese family. There is a huge inscription of dedication which fascinates every visitor as it portrays the history as well as psychology of Renaissance period. The marble decorations, semicircular archways, etc make it very attractive.

Restaurants & shopping: The neighborhood of both the regions is quite calm and goes about their functions with an unnoticeable style. This style is reflected in promoting restaurants & shopping centers. There are many restaurants available but are barely promotional; similar is the case with shopping spots which are sedate yet offer compassionate welcome to their customers.

10. EUR

Primarily, EUR district is residential in nature with a lot of businesses' focusing on future development. Nonetheless, the district is home for some modern monuments built during the progress of this region.

The Palace of Italian Civilization stands as major symbol for EUR district. Furthermore, it also symbolizes the fascism prevalent during the 20th century; in fact this monument is esteemed high as fascistic architecture. It is often referred to as the "square coliseum".

The piazza of Marconi is a popular place with detailed stone sculpted obelisk that shines throughout the day depicting fascinating information through the form of images.

The Ardeatine Caves is a place of memorial cemetery which unfortunately became the execution spot for 335 people during the Resistance. However, the historic appeal of the caves is not lost and many people visit this place annually.

The National Museum of the middle Ages contains different artworks done by artists ranging from 6th century AD to post-classic era. The museum highlights the lifestyle and growth of Roman citizens along with its country through centuries of modifications.

Restaurants & shopping: As mentioned before EUR is a business area making it necessary for development of restaurants and shopping centers. In addition, there are many hotels for accommodation like Hotel ibis Styles which come at reasonable prices.

11. Via Vittorio Veneto

Interestingly, this is not a region but is one of the most famous and expensive streets of Rome. The street acquired its name in memory of Vittorio Veneto battle that took place during the 20th century.

The Church of Santa Maria dell Concezione of the Capuchins resembles gothic architecture; however, it has a fascinating pious story of Capuchin friars who decided to preserve the remains of their dead brothers by decorating the crypt walls with their bones. They believed this would make others understand the nature of human life which is transitory. There are many highlights in this church which cannot be missed while travelling Rome. The church is the only reason for mentioning Via Veneto.

12. Ostiense and San Paolo

Ostiense and its surrounding regions are famous and well admired for their magnificent murals spread all around and most of them are visible from roads. However, every mural is a masterpiece and not be missed; therefore take considerable time while travelling in Ostiense and Garbatella. In addition, there are many famous film locations used in famous movies.

The pyramid of Cestius is enthralling to watch as the visitors feel two great civilizations are merged in one place. The experience is indescribable for many who are versed with Egyptian and Roman civilizations. Furthermore, near to the pyramid is a protestant cemetery **Cimitero Acattolico** which is the resting place of history's most renowned poets, historians, etc.

Basilica of St. Paul's is one of the four papal basilicas of Roman Christianity which attracts a lot of attention from visitors, theologians, historians, etc. After St. Peter's Basilica this is the second largest papal Basilica built over the burial place of Paul, the Apostle. The

Basilica is present in San Paolo outside the walls in Italian jurisdiction.

Restaurants & shopping: For shopping enthusiasts and food lovers there is no crisis for finding such desired destinations. Ristorante San Paolo is known for its authentic Italian recipes given out for reasonable prices. Shopping is within reach with wide variety of complexes for those shopaholics.

13. Pigneto and San Lorenzo

Pigneto is pretty much built in the form a triangle extending between Via Prenestina, Via dell' Acqua Bullicante, Via Casilina from Piazzale Labicano. There are long rows of Pine trees along the region which captivates the eye of the visitors. San Lorenzo is a deviation for the visitor from historic and traditional burst of knowledge as it is famous for nightlife, clubs and bars, etc. In between these regions there are many murals on walls created by well recognized artists.

The cemetery of Verano is the main cemetery of Rome where it is believed every family has an ancestor buried with the exception of noble families, cardinals and Popes. Furthermore, the cemetery also contains great historic personalities and iconic individuals who paved way for the development of Rome.

Restaurants & shopping: Fast paced life of present civilization meets its match in these regions as people are trendy, adaptive, and recognize the visitor's needs unconditionally. Therefore, tourists can find divergent options for food, accommodation and shopping.

14. Monti and Esquilino

Monti region is near the Coliseum yet most visitors who are new to Rome skip this place without having knowledge of the place. However, frequent visitors do not want to miss out as the place is flooded with antiquity. There are many piazzas (like Piazza degli Zingari and Piazza della Madonna dei Monti) which unnoticeably drain time with entertainment and fun. Esquilono is near the Termini railway station and the in between regions are studded with murals along the road.

The Church of Santa Maria in Monti is dedicated to Virgin Mary has extravagant frescoes in its dome which makes it a famous tourist destination. The famous altarpiece of Madonna with Child and St. Charles Borrmeo is found in this church.

The Basilica of Santa Maria Maggiore (Our Lady of the Snow) in Esquilino is the biggest Marian Catholic Church in the city of Rome dedicated to Madonna. It is the only church representing Christian architecture of the early ages.

Esquilino is regarded as the multiethnic district of Rome, the reason being the presence of extensive market area providing huge varieties of items exported from all over the world. Therefore, most visitors with different languages and customs flock this area.

Restaurants & shopping: Interestingly, though near the Termini railway station Esquilino provides cheap lodging for the tourists. In addition, due to multiethnic customs there are many hotels, restaurants and shopping destinations which provide things for reasonable prices. Especially, Esquilino has Indian, Chinese, Japanese restaurants along with traditional native spots which makes it a favorite place for food lovers.

15. Salario and Trieste

Salario is a residential area known for its parks which are very pleasant with great atmosphere. These parks organize many music festivals annually to attract visitors. Trieste is towards the north-eastern side which offers a fair surprise to the tourists.

Villa Ada and **Villa Torlonia** are among the richest parks in Rome in terms of bio-diversity. Visitors feel like floating on the green bed of Nature with intense calmness and inner peace. A stroll in either of these parks will uplift the mood of any individual.

Macro is Rome's contemporary art museum with a panorama of works done by modern artists. In addition, there are public zones and service centers inside the vast region which facilitates ease of movement of visitors.

Quartiere Coppedè literally stuns the visitors with its 17 villas and 26 mini palazzos with hybrid architecture including Medieval, Greek, Gothic, Italian, Baroque and Art Deco works. The Frogs' fountain, Building of the spider, Fairies' building are literally impregnated with grandiose art work.

Restaurants & shopping: Salario and Trieste being crowded by tourists offer many shopping locations and restaurants. Ristorante Eleonora D'Arborea, Il Viaggio, Gel' Istria, Al Ceppo, Capo Boi are well known restaurants in these regions.

16. San Giovanni

San Giovanni is most approachable through the Appian Way and is one of the most crowded districts among Rome. The district is embedded with fine murals and holy regions.

The Basilica of St. John Lateran is considered to be the Mother of all churches around the world. This is the fourth of the major basilicas which complete the chain of four; the other being Basilicas of St. Peter's, St. Paul's and Maria of Esquilino. St. John's basilica reflects eras of Christian faith and progression made by the religion through generations of conflict.

The Holy Stairs or **Scala Santa** - holy stairs brought to Rome during the 4th century; these are believed to be the original steps ascended by Jesus Christ in the famous Pontius Pilate's palace of Jerusalem. Devotees ascend these stairs on knees showing their faith and offer prayers in the same position. The magnanimity of this region is very huge and not to be missed by any visitor regardless of their belief.

Restaurants & shopping: The clothing market in San Giovanni is famous for giving out Roman traditional attires for low prices. In addition, there are normal fittings and boutique styled clothes available in the cloth market. Pizzeria Luzzi and Charly's Saucière are among the many famous restaurants in the province of San Giovanni.

17. Ostia

Ostia is a fair distance away from the Vatican and offers a completely different lifestyle and customs due to its existence near the seashore. There are many beachside hotels which offer a refreshing view for those who ardently involved themselves in understanding the greatness of Rome. However, there are several historical sites which are associated with enthralling stories.

The Roman theatre of Ancient Ostia is a famous archeological excavation site with a before Christ era theatre. The complex is majestic for the vision even today and hosts many events, concerts, etc.

Archeological park of Ancient Ostia is a vast archeological site which the tourists cannot afford to miss. The ancient history and architecture are illuminated through findings from this site. The history is remarkable and connects various eras of rule. The castle of Julius II stands with glory among the picturesque village area of the past.

Restaurants & shopping: Ostia is the center for many resorts and the seaside is famous for its attractive tourist accommodations. Travelers need not worry about anything when in Ostia as it tends their every need.

Part 2. Night Life in Rome

Rome is different from many other places across the world, even in case of nightlife as well. Normally, night life starts at 7 or 8, but when it comes to Rome, it starts at around 10. Yes, you are going to enjoy your night life here in Rome, really late. You will not find it really difficult to find the most interesting clubs and pubs in Rome, but what may seem more interesting for you in Rome is, people spend their nightlife more outdoors and not at these pubs. But, let us add another point here, you will not find any pub, disco or night club free. They are always full of people enjoy loud music. Here are a few interesting and really loud places for you to enjoy night life. Pub Crawl, Campo dei Fiori, Piazza Gathering, Testaccio, Ice Club, Jonathan's Angels, Trinity college, Grotta Pinta Lounge, Vineria Reggio Wine Bar, On The Rox, Nag's Head Pub, Hard Rock Café, San Lorenzo and many more.

Conclusion

In conclusion, Rome captivates the soul as well as the heart of visitors with its magnificent culture, diverse landscapes, architectural brilliance, religious benevolence, and more. The golden rays of Rome will never cease to mystify the beholder making them to say with awe struck mind - "I came, I saw, I wondered."

Thank You Page

I want to personally thank you for reading my book. I hope you found information in this book useful and I would be very grateful if you could leave your honest review about this book. I certainly want to thank you in advance for doing this.

If you have the time, you can check my other books too.